OSCEOLA
PATRIOT AND WARRIOR

OSCEOLA
PATRIOT AND WARRIOR

by **MOSES JUMPER**
and **BEN SONDER**
Alex Haley, General Editor

Illustrations by Patrick Soper

RAINTREE STECK-VAUGHN
P U B L I S H E R S
The Steck-Vaughn Company

Austin, Texas

Published by Steck-Vaughn Company.

Text, illustrations, and cover art copyright © 1993 by Dialogue Systems, Inc., 627 Broadway, New York, New York 10012. All rights reserved.

Cover art by Patrick Soper

Printed in the United States of America

7 8 9 10 11 12   LB   01   00

Library of Congress Cataloging-in-Publication Data

Jumper, Moses. 1950–
  Osceola, patriot and warrior / by Moses Jumper and Ben
Sonder: illustrations by Pat Soper
    p.   cm.—(Stories of America)
  Summary: Describes the struggle of Seminole chief and war-
rior Osceola to save his people from being forced off their land in
Florida.
    ISBN 0-8114-7225-6 (hardcover) — ISBN 0-8114-8065-8
(softcover)
    1. Osceola, Seminole chief, 1804–1838—Juvenile literature.
2. Seminole Indians—Biography—Juvenile literature. 3. Seminole
Indians—Wars—Juvenile literature. [1. Osceola, Seminole chief,
1804–1838. 2. Seminole Indians —Biography. 3. Indians of North
America—Biography.] I. Sonder, Ben, 1954–. II. Soper, Patrick,
ill. III. Title. IV. Series.
E99.S280825   1993
973'.0497302—dc20
                                                    92-25209
[B]   CIP
                                                    AC

ISBN 0-8114-7225-6 (Hardcover)
ISBN 0-8114-8065-8 (Softcover)

The authors would like to thank Rick Larios for his guidance and Jim Ciment for his assistance with the research for this book.

A Note About Alex Haley

Osceola, Patriot and Warrior is one of two books in the *Stories of America* series completed after the death of Alex Haley in February 1992.

Despite his involvement in a number of other projects, Mr. Haley found the time to guide the formation of the *Stories of America*. As General Editor, he provided editorial direction through all stages of book development. And for each of the 26 books completed prior to his death, he wrote a special introduction.

Alex Haley was an inspiration to all of us involved in the project. We did our best to carry on in his spirit. We hope that readers will find evidence of Alex Haley's influence on these pages, just as we felt his influence while completing them.

The *Stories of America* series is Alex Haley's contribution to the education of America's young people. This book is respectfully dedicated to his memory.

Introduction

The United States wanted the Seminoles out of Florida. Their removal would free Florida for white settlement. It would also protect slavery in the United States because runaway slaves had frequently escaped to Florida to live among the Seminoles.

The Seminoles, however, fought to keep their land and their freedom. They were joined by African Americans who were also fighting for their freedom. The two were allies in a War for Independence that wasn't much different from the one that had granted the United States its freedom fifty years earlier.

The story of Osceola and the Second Seminole War is a special tale of freedom. It is a story that shows us how much courage and determination is needed to begin a battle that might prove impossible to win. And it reminds us that those who have such courage and determination are true heroes.

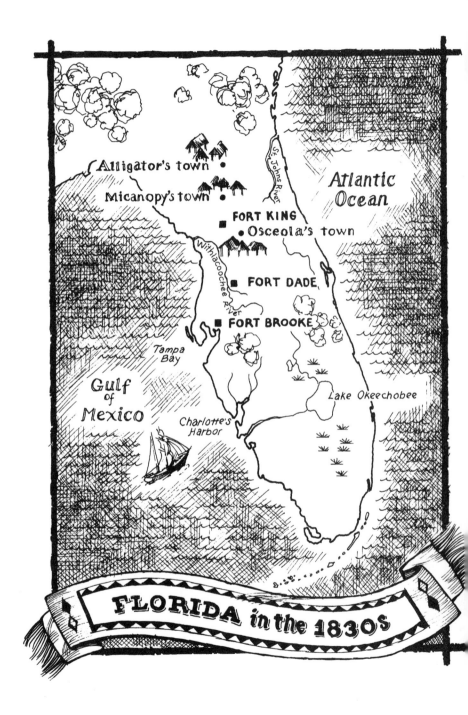

FLORIDA in the 1830s

CONTENTS

THE RUNAWAY

Osceola, the Seminole war chief, lay on his belly on the black earth without moving a hair. His ears, trained to hear the slightest sound in the forest, listened. Something was moving in the distance. The sound came to him muffled by the dense jungle of wild oak trees. It was a dull, crashing sound, like a wild boar—or an enemy.

Osceola pressed closer to the warm earth and listened harder. The sound was getting nearer, moving toward him.

Osceola turned to peer at his village. It lay across the creek, in a clearing a hundred steps behind him. Everything looked peaceful in the still, bright air. Smoke from a fire rose straight up through the leaves of a live oak. The corner of a hut made of palmetto branches was reflected in the slow rippling creek.

Then the crashing sound grew closer, louder. The dogs that guarded the village began barking. Osceola sprang to a crouching position. He stayed low in the brush, his rifle ready in his hands. Sweat dripped from his forehead.

The leaves parted. Osceola raised the rifle and pointed it as a human form tumbled toward him. Then he lowered it. The man, who was barefoot and shirtless, had stumbled and collapsed. Slowly he struggled to get up. He was exhausted.

Osceola knew at once that the man was a runaway slave, probably from one of the nearby sugar plantations. Desperate for freedom, he had fled into the hot, humid swamps of Central Florida.

The runaway had no weapons with him—nothing to protect him or help him hunt for food. He had probably been living on berries and the occasional squirrel he could trap. From the looks of him, he had also fallen several times. His ankles, chest, and even his face were caked with mud. His body was covered with the bites of mosquitoes and chiggers.

The black man's sudden arrival was nothing new to Osceola. Blacks had been living with the Seminoles for at least fifty years, maybe more. A number lived in Osceola's village. In recent years, word had spread among the plantation slaves that life with the Seminoles was far better than life under their white owners.

Whether slave or free, blacks were accepted as members of the Seminole community. They farmed the land, hunted, and even married Seminole women and men. Many dressed like Seminoles in long leather stockings and feathered turbans. On the plantations blacks were slaves, and slaves were property. Owners could treat them however they wanted; slaves had no rights.

The runaway struggled to his knees. He stared at Osceola, wondering whether he would help him, ignore him, or kill him. He needed the

Seminole's help. Slowly, he pointed to his mouth. He opened it and made chewing motions. He was telling Osceola that he was hungry. His eyes begged Osceola to help him.

Osceola, a man of enormous strength, pulled the runaway slave to his feet. He quickly and easily lifted him onto his back. With the exhausted man clinging to him, Osceola waded into the creek. Its warm waters rippled about his knees as his feet sank into the black mud.

Mosquitoes buzzed around Osceola as he climbed the other bank of the creek. But they did not bite him. Before going out, Osceola had smeared his skin with bear grease to prevent insect bites.

Near the creek, two Seminole women sat by a small fire. A side of venison lay on a dried deerskin. Game had been very scarce that year. But Osceola himself had spotted and killed this deer the morning before.

The women had cut pieces of the venison and wrapped them in leaves. Now the wrapped pieces sat steaming in the hot coals.

Osceola lowered the runaway to the grass and asked the two women to feed him. One of them rose and bent toward the fire. With a stick she dragged out a piece of the wrapped venison. She used the pointed end of the stick to poke through the leaves and pull out the meat. Then she wrapped it in a piece of bread made of sweetbriar root. During the last hard winter, the sweetbriar root had been all that some members of the tribe could find to eat.

Wordlessly the Seminole woman offered the wrapped deer meat to the black man. He took it from her, blew on it to cool it off, and hungrily began to eat. Between bites he smiled gratefully at the two women.

Except for the sound of the man's hurried chewing, there was silence. The smell of Spanish moss mingled with the smell of the wood smoke and the roasting meat. Osceola rose and walked toward the corn fields and the palmetto huts. He wanted to find Abraham. Abraham was a black Seminole. He had lived among the Seminoles for years and would be Osceola's interpreter.

Nearer the huts Osceola saw a small group of

boys playing. They were spinning tops on a piece of stretched deerskin. They tried to get as many tops spinning at one time as possible. Each top was made from a root called "deerfood." The fat root was pierced with a sharp stick on which the top spun.

The boys laughed as the tops whirled and wobbled on the deerskin blanket but then suddenly grew silent when they noticed the powerful war chief standing over them. Osceola addressed them, his voice deep and serious. He wanted to know if they had seen Abraham. One of them pointed to the other side of the village.

Abraham, wearing only his knee pants, sat in the grass outside a palmetto hut. Even sitting down he looked tall and lean. He was cleaning an animal skin with a long hunting knife. Beads of sweat formed on his high, broad forehead. His good eye squinted at his work in the bright afternoon sunlight. The other eye could not see very well. For years it had been clouded over by a growth that allowed only a small amount of light to pass through.

Osceola asked Abraham to come to the creek

to talk with the runaway. Lately the number of runaway slaves seeking refuge with the Seminoles had been increasing. Abraham knew that this angered many of the white planters in the area. Although he was glad when any slave found freedom, he was also worried that the angry whites might cause new trouble. Relations with the whites were already bad enough.

When Osceola returned with Abraham, the runaway struggled to his feet. He begged Abraham to convince Osceola to keep him in the village. He had been pursued by slave-catchers for two days before finally losing them in the swamp.

Abraham interpreted the man's words for Osceola, who stood studying the runaway. Osceola knew that the United States governor of Florida had ordered all Seminoles to return runaways to their white owners. But through Abraham he told the runaway that he had no intention of doing so.

The man gave a sigh of relief and sat back down.

Just then a strange sound filtered through the oak trees. The runaway gazed around warily. What was that? The sound echoed again through the forest. It was the blare of a bugle.

Abraham explained that there were soldiers nearby. Panic clouded the runaway's face. Were soldiers searching for him? He rose to his feet as if to run back into the swamp.

Abraham shook his head. The soldiers had been there for some time. In fact, they had built a fort just a few miles from the village. Tomorrow, a large delegation of Seminoles would be going there to talk with the whites.

The runaway was suspicious. He, too, knew how angry the whites were about slaves escaping to live with the Seminoles. Was that what they would be meeting about? Would the Seminoles betray him to the slave-catchers?

Abraham translated the runaway's questions, but Osceola only shrugged his shoulders.

Abraham explained to the runaway that that was only one of the things to be discussed at the meeting. The whites wanted runaway slaves returned, but they also wanted the Seminoles out of Florida. They hoped to move the Seminoles to other, faraway lands. Then Florida would belong to the whites. The white government did not understand that the land belonged only to the Giver of Breath. Anyone could use it, but no one owned it except the Giver of Breath.

Abraham explained further. Twelve years earlier the Treaty of Moultrie Creek had ended a war between the whites and the Seminoles. This treaty with the United States government forced the Seminoles to give up more than 28 million acres of land to the whites. They had to move onto the 4 million acres they now occupied.

Then, five years ago, the President of the United States had signed a law that would require the Seminoles to move out of Florida entirely, into the Arkansas Territory. Some Seminole leaders had agreed to this, and another treaty had been signed. But many Seminoles were against the move.

Tomorrow the Seminoles would meet with the whites at the new fort. A man named Wiley

Thompson would be there as an agent of the United States government. He had already held a meeting with the Seminoles earlier today and it had gone badly. It had ended with a white officer threatening the Seminoles with forced removal. Tomorrow they were to tell Thompson whether they would move peacefully or not.

The runaway wanted to know what the Seminoles had decided. Abraham translated the question.

Osceola said nothing. But his jaw hardened, and his fingers curled around the handle of his hunting knife.

═◆═ 2 ═◆═

TO KEEP THEIR HOMES

The next day, three miles from the Seminole village, Wiley Thompson stood atop a grassy hill overlooking a forest and a lake. Behind him rose the twenty-foot-high wooden fence of Fort King. Crammed inside the fort were officers' quarters, barracks, kitchens, mess halls, and stores of ammunition.

It was early morning on April 23, 1835. The sun was rising over the pines below. The air still had a slight chill. In just a few short hours the Seminole leaders would be arriving to discuss their removal to Arkansas.

Thompson was worried about the meeting. Two years before, several Seminole chiefs, including Jumper and Black Dirt, had gone to Arkansas to inspect the land to which the American government expected the Seminoles to move. Abraham had gone along as their interpreter. The land had looked good for farming and raising cattle, but the winters there were harsh. Worse, the Creeks, who were old enemies of the Seminoles, controlled the land they would live on. None of the chiefs had liked this.

However, after much pressure from the whites, some of the visiting Seminoles, including Abraham, had signed a paper. As the chiefs understood it, the paper said only that they had seen the land and that they would put the question of moving before the entire Seminole nation. Then the nation would decide for itself whether or not to move.

But, when the chiefs had returned to Florida, they were surprised to learn that the paper said something different to the United States government. It was claiming that the signatures on the paper meant that the Seminoles had already agreed to go to Arkansas. Government officals wanted to set a date for the move as soon as possible.

Some of the chiefs who had signed began preparing with their families and followers for the move. But Abraham, Jumper, and the others were outraged. They charged that someone had changed the wording of the document after they had signed it. Someone had tricked them. They and most of their followers vowed to resist moving to Arkansas.

Thompson wondered how far the disagreement over the treaty would go. Yesterday he had tried his best to convince those against the treaty to accept it. But the meeting went so badly, he had lost his temper. General Duncan L. Clinch, the military commander of Florida, had also become enraged and threatened the Seminoles. They would move peacefully, he had roared, or his troops would make them move.

Now, beneath the hill on which Thompson stood, a group of soldiers were training in the woods. They were learning how to fight in the dense underbrush. It was hoped that they would learn to move through it with as much skill as the Seminoles could.

The Seminoles knew the mossy forests and swamps of this country well. They could move through the palmetto leaves, hanging vines, and cypress stumps much faster than the soldiers. They knew how to use the leaves, vines, and grass for cover. They could shoot arrows through the tangled tree branches and hit their mark. The dense forest never slowed them down.

Thompson saw the soldiers moving clumsily through the underbrush. Because it was still cool, they wore heavy coats over their blue uniforms. Each time they needed to reload their guns, they had to reach under their coats for ammunition. This took precious time. He knew that the Seminoles were faster. In times of war, each warrior carried a rifle ball ready in his mouth. While the white troops were still fumbling with their buttons, the Seminoles would be firing a second round.

Thompson watched as the soldiers tripped on vines or stubbed their toes on cypress stumps. He heard their curses as they slapped at mosquitoes. Thompson turned away in disgust. The soldiers weren't nearly ready. And there was little time left to get them ready.

Thompson knew that the year had been a bad one for the Seminoles. The winter temperatures had plunged below freezing. The weather had stayed cold into the spring and crops died soon after sprouting. Game had all but disappeared. Many Seminoles had gone hungry. Some had very nearly starved to death. And almost all the Seminoles blamed their hardships on the Treaty of Moultrie Creek. It had left them with land that was poor for farming and poor for hunting.

To survive, a few Seminoles had raided nearby plantations and stolen cattle. There had also been other trouble. On several occasions, slave traders had raided Seminole towns hoping to capture escaped slaves. The traders seized every black man, woman, or child they had found, runaway or not. The runaways were returned to their owners; everyone else was sold into slavery.

Thompson was alarmed at all the trouble. The only good news was that more troops were on their way to Fort King. They would be needed if war came. And with each passing day it seemed more and more likely that war was coming.

At about 11:00 A.M., several hundred Seminoles began arriving. On the grounds inside the fort, Thompson and General Clinch sat on a wooden platform built ten feet off the ground. The soldiers feared the chiggers and snakes of this region and wanted to be above the grass.

Thompson fixed his eyes on the Seminole leaders as they filed into the fort. They had threaded their long, dark hair with feathers. Their eyebrows had been dyed black. Red paint formed half circles under their eyes. Some chiefs had silver rings in their noses, and their tunics were covered with hammered circles of silver. Below their tunics, their beaded sashes sparkled in the sunlight.

Finally everyone was assembled. The chiefs sat on or near the platform with Thompson and

Clinch. Over a thousand Seminole men and women sat on the grass. A few naked babies crawled among them. At some distance stood a troop of armed soldiers, ready in case trouble should come sooner than was expected.

Despite the importance of the occasion, Micanopy, one of the Seminoles' great chiefs, was absent. He had sent word through Jumper that he was not feeling well. Thompson was suspicious about the excuse. On other occasions Micanopy had shown strong opposition to the move. Thompson wondered whether Micanopy was really sick. Maybe he was absent because he wanted to show everyone that he had no respect for the treaty or for Thompson. The thought was enough to color Thompson's face with anger.

Jumper, though, had been asked to speak for Micanopy. Thompson nodded for him to begin. Jumper slowly began to explain Micanopy's position. From time to time, he paused so that Abraham could translate his words for Thompson and Clinch.

He explained that the treaty that had been

signed in Arkansas did not speak for the entire Seminole nation. Micanopy, he said, was firmly against the Seminoles leaving Florida. And so were many others. Their ancestors and their ancestors' ancestors were buried in Florida soil. The Seminoles would rather die than move from their homes.

But Thompson wasn't listening very closely. Instead, his attention was focused on a handsome Seminole with a long straight nose and a serious, fixed stare. The man was standing rather than sitting, and his arms were crossed tightly over his powerful chest.

"Watch that man," Thompson whispered to General Clinch. "He has great influence." The man he pointed to was Osceola.

When Jumper finished speaking, Thompson stood up. From a table he picked up a paper. With Abraham translating, Thompson began to read it aloud. The paper said that the Seminoles would now agree to the terms of the treaty signed in Arkansas and would soon move out of Florida.

Thompson read the paper as if there was nothing at all to discuss. As far as he was concerned, the move to Arkansas was a closed case. As he spoke, impatience and even a bit of anger could be heard in his voice.

He announced that he would give the Seminoles more time to move—until January 15, 1836. That would give them about eight and a half months to make preparations. Thompson thought the extra time would please the Seminoles. He believed he was being more than fair.

Thompson put the paper on the table. "Who will sign?" he asked.

Eight chiefs nodded reluctantly. They would sign. These chiefs knew what would happen if they refused to sign: a war with the whites that would cost many lives. They preferred to make a new life in Arkansas rather than to risk such hardships. After hesitating a moment, they walked unhappily to the table and signed.

But four other chiefs shook their heads no.

And these chiefs were among the most powerful of the Seminole leaders. They were Alligator, Arpeika, Black Dirt, and Jumper.

Red with fury, Thompson asked Jumper again, "Where is Micanopy?"

"Sick," replied Alligator.

"I don't believe it!" screamed Thompson. "He's just shunning his responsibility. Jumper, will you tell us whether or not Micanopy intends to honor the treaty?"

Alligator, Black Dirt, and Arpeika fixed their eyes on Jumper and shook their heads.

"He will not honor the treaty," Jumper finally said.

As if he were about to punish misbehaving children, Thompson grabbed a pen. He began to read from another paper. It was a list of all the Seminole chiefs. When he came to the names of Micanopy, Jumper, Alligator, Black Dirt, and Arpeika, he crossed out each name.

"These men no longer represent the Seminole nation!" he shouted. The thousand or so

Seminole people present gasped in disbelief when Thompson's words were translated. No white man had the right to take such an action!

Thompson began reading the names of other important Seminoles. Some came to the table and signed, but others stayed rooted in their seats.

Arguments broke out among the Seminole men and women sitting on the grass. Some felt that everyone in the nation should refuse to move, regardless of papers, signatures, or past agreements. Others felt that such an attitude would bring war. Thompson's behavior was proof that he was willing to go to war to drive the Seminoles out. Perhaps the whites were too powerful to resist.

Finally Osceola's name was called. Slowly the tall warrior unfolded his arms. He paused for a moment, then walked gracefully to the table on which the document lay. He leaned forward across the table. In a soft, sure voice, he said, "We don't want an agent. This land is ours." Then

instead of reaching for the pen, he drew his hunting knife. Lifting it into the air, he sank it into the table with enormous force.

"This is the only way I sign!" he thundered in Seminole. The gesture didn't require translation.

A great cry of approval rang forth from some Seminole warriors. Others shouted their disapproval of Osceola's angry gesture. In the midst of the uproar, Osceola walked calmly away.

❖ 3 ❖

THE IMPRISONED WARRIOR

Immediately after Osceola had plunged his knife into the table at Fort King, he began planning to resist the order to move. He had a bare eight months before the United States army would try to force the Seminoles to leave Florida. That meant there was no time to waste.

Osceola, Jumper, Arpeika, and a small band of followers began making frequent visits to white trading posts. Here they traded animal skins for supplies of guns, powder, and lead. Abraham, who was worried about the safety of the black Seminoles, began collecting arms as well. He bought many through free blacks and Spanish fishermen living in Florida.

It was not long before Wiley Thompson noticed the increased purchases of arms and gunpowder by the Seminoles. The whole situation made him nervous. He knew that some Seminoles were buying these supplies in preparation for their move to Arkansas. They would need the guns and powder and lead for hunting. But he was also certain that others wanted the arms to carry out a violent resistance to the move.

Panicking, Thompson quickly outlawed the selling of all arms to all Seminoles, regardless of their reasons for wanting them. Osceola was furious. Abraham was angry as well. Without arms, they wouldn't be able to defend their lands or their freedom. First the slave traders would come to claim the black Seminoles as runaways. Then the army would ship everyone else to Arkansas like a herd of sheep.

At Fort King, Wiley Thompson sat at his desk, bent over some routine paperwork. At times, his mind wandered to more important matters. He was worried about the difficulties ahead. It occurred to him that punishing those Seminole leaders who were most against the move might serve as an example to the rest. It was an idea to consider.

Outside Thompson's door, shirtless soldiers worked in the hot sun with hammers and saws. They were rebuilding a broken panel in the fort wall. Thompson listened to the pounding of the hammers and the hum of the saws. Then another sound broke through. It was the sound of approaching footsteps.

Suddenly the door swung open with a bang. Standing before him was Osceola. The war chief was dressed as if for a formal occasion. He wore a knee-length coat with a floral design. A colorful sash tied it at the waist. And he had set a fresh feather in his turban.

Osceola knew only a little English, but he managed to make his thoughts clear to Thompson. "I am told I may not buy arms and powder," he said.

"That's right. Not at this time," answered

Thompson, without a word of explanation or a hint of apology.

Osceola asked Thompson how the Seminoles were to hunt without guns or ammunition. He demanded to know by what right Thompson was interfering in Seminole business.

Thompson stared haughtily at him. He seemed not to have the slightest interest in Osceola's protest.

Osceola grew angry. "Am I a slave?" he bellowed at Thompson. "I am a Seminole!"

Thompson did not respond. Instead he tightened his lips into a smug half-smile and shrugged his shoulders.

Osceola flew into a rage. If the white leader had no respect for him, then why should he respect the white leader? "I will make the white man red with blood," he threatened. Then he strode out of the office.

Thompson was enraged. No man had ever spoken to him in his office in that tone of voice before. From now on, he would keep an even closer eye on every move Osceola made.

A few months later, Osceola again encountered Thompson at the fort. Neither man had changed his opinion of the other. Their meeting did not go well. At one point, words between the two men grew so hot that Osceola pulled out his knife and waved it in the air before Thompson's face. Then he departed. Thompson walked quickly after him. At the door he called to Colonel Fanning, who was standing nearby.

"Colonel, will you arrest that man!" said Thompson.

Four soldiers were immediately sent after Osceola. When they caught up with him, he turned and sent one of them crashing to the ground. The other three soldiers, however, overpowered Osceola and dragged him to the guardhouse. They put him in irons and locked him in a guardhouse cell. The heavy iron shackles tore at his wrists and ankles.

Throughout the evening Osceola shouted threats at Thompson. Being put in shackles was the worst insult a Seminole could endure. And imprisoning a warrior chief was unthinkable among his people. He swore revenge on Thompson.

Hours passed and evening came. But the war chief's angry cries did not stop. Soldiers tossed and turned in their beds, unable to sleep. The howls of the warrior sent a chill down everyone's spine. Few, if any, understood the Seminole words Osceola shouted. But the anger and menace in them was understood by all.

Finally, at midnight, the noise stopped abruptly. An eerie silence took over. One by one, the soldiers fell asleep.

Osceola's anger had lessened, and he was able to think clearly. He spent the entire night working out a plan of escape. In the morning, he would tell Thompson that he was sorry. He would say anything necessary to be released. He would even sign a paper saying that he agreed with the treaties. The important thing was to get out. Then he could continue his efforts to keep his people in Florida. Later he would get his revenge on Thompson.

When morning came Osceola sent his apologies. Thompson, feeling satisfied, accepted them. In his view, the Seminole had lost his temper and acted unwisely, childishly even. But he felt he had shown Osceola a firm hand and had taught him a lesson. Perhaps his punishment would now serve as an example to other rebellious Seminoles. He ordered Osceola released immediately.

The guardhouse cell was unlocked. The shackles were removed from Osceola's reddened wrists and ankles. But as Osceola walked quietly out of the fort, Colonel Fanning came to see Thompson in his office.

"You've made a mistake, General," said Fanning. "That man should never have been turned loose. He's your enemy for life."

Thompson scoffed at the idea. He said smugly that he had shown Osceola it didn't pay to trifle with him. He was sure the warrior would be no further trouble. Thompson stood up and opened the door of the office. Bright June light filled the room. The shriek of a wild turkey in the woods was heard over the fort's lowing cattle.

Suddenly another shrill cry pierced the air. Thompson recognized it immediately. It was Osceola's war cry coming from the woods.

4

THE WAR BEGINS

Immediately upon returning from the fort, Osceola called a meeting with Micanopy, Jumper, Abraham, and others. He described his imprisonment by Thompson. "Brothers," Osceola declared, "we must finish our preparations. We should be ready to fight during the last moon of this year."

Abraham listened carefully to Osceola's words. He, for one, was more ready than ever to take action. In recent months, slave traders had increased their raiding of Seminole towns and villages. Only by fighting together could the

Seminoles remain on their land and the blacks remain free.

In October 1835, about 1,500 Seminoles met secretly in a part of Central Florida called the Big Swamp. At this meeting, the war chiefs revealed their plans for resistance. They called for all Seminoles to refuse to move to Arkansas.

"Brothers," said Osceola, "I have said before that if any of our people want to go west, we won't permit it. They are our enemies, and they must be treated as enemies. I say that anyone who prepares to move must be killed by the nation."

Some disagreed with Osceola's words. They were still planning to move to Arkansas. But they stayed silent, fearing Osceola and his followers. Then a large number stood and pledged themselves to the struggle to remain in Florida. They vowed to fight to the death if necessary for their rights.

That same month, war between the whites and the Seminoles began with a few small skirmishes. Meanwhile Abraham visited the sugar plantations in Central and Eastern Florida. At each one he would wait in the forest or swamp until the masters of the plantations were away or sleeping. Then he would talk to the slaves. He urged them to join the Seminoles, offering them freedom in return. Many accepted Abraham's offer. In addition, free blacks living in Florida also agreed to become allies with the Seminoles.

An alarmed General Clinch made a desperate call to Washington for more troops. Several new forts were built in Central Florida. And into these forts poured many white settlers who feared for their lives.

The Seminoles were busy finishing their preparations. Now, after weeks of training their warriors, Osceola and the other war leaders were ready. They planned a brilliant series of attacks throughout Central and Eastern Florida. Together, the attacks were meant to send a message to the United States government: *No matter the cost, we will fight to keep our lands.*

Like Wiley Thompson, General Clinch was aware of the Seminoles' superior fighting skill.

What neither he nor Thompson suspected was how well organized and how determined their resistance would be. That would become painfully clear to both men late in December. But the first to learn this hard truth was a troop of soldiers commanded by Major Francis L. Dade.

Dade's men left Fort Brooke to relieve the troops at Fort King on December 23. A cold rain slowed them down. Their heavy coats were soaked with icy water and their fingers were numb with cold. The forty-mile march seemed much longer in the bad weather.

On Christmas Day the soldiers came to a small river. Major Dade, seeing that the bridge had been burned by the Seminoles, motioned for his troops to wade through the freezing water. Teeth chattering, the soldiers walked one by one into the river. A raft was built to carry their heavy cannon across. When the cannon fell into the shallow river, it took the soldiers hours to lift it out of the mud.

Three days later the rain stopped but the weather turned even colder. A strong wind blew

from the north. After a breakfast of pork rind and stale biscuits, the soldiers continued to plow through the bushes and tangled roots of the forest. Finally, they came to a heavy thicket of palmetto trees bordered on one side by a pond. Behind the palmettos was a pine forest.

What no one knew was that the forest on the right hid a small army of Seminole warriors. Led by Jumper and Alligator, they had followed the soldiers for days. Osceola had instructed Jumper and Alligator to stay as close to Dade as possible, and to attack when the time was right. And now, according to Jumper, the time was right.

As the soldiers stood in the thicket, still only halfway to their destination, Major Dade made an announcement. "We have now got through all danger," he said. "Keep up a good heart, and when we get to Fort King, I'll give you three days for Christmas."

Then a shot rang out. No one knew from where it had come. But Major Dade fell forward. His body slid off his horse and into the mud. He had been killed by Micanopy, who had joined the war party in time to signal the battle's start.

Immediately, the sound of gunfire filled the forest. Within seconds, half the soldiers were hit.

"Take cover!" shouted a captain. Those soldiers who could still run dashed behind palmetto trees. Those too severely wounded to run crawled for cover. Several soldiers tried hurriedly to load the cannon, but they were shot down. Others scrambled to replace them. Gunfire and cries of pain echoed in the swamp. The smoke from the gunfire clouded the battlefield.

The cannon boomed, sending several rounds crashing into the forest. Its fire, however, did little damage, while the soldiers who manned it were cut down one after the other. Out of the original 108 white soldiers, there were soon barely 30 left alive. None of the Seminoles had yet been killed and only a few wounded.

After three hours of fighting, Jumper signalled for the Seminoles to withdraw. The battleground was suddenly quiet. After waiting for several minutes to make sure that the Seminoles had withdrawn, the soldiers hurriedly chopped down trees to build a barricade. Soon a triangular fence only two or three feet high was completed.

Several soldiers then crept out on their hands and knees to the cannon. They dragged the cannon back to the fence and began to load it. During all this activity, the forest was quiet. The soldiers, huddled low behind the barricade, waited for the battle to resume. They watched nervously for any signs of movement in the forest. It stayed quiet for almost an hour. The quiet, too, was frightening.

While the soldiers were building their low fort, the Seminoles had removed their wounded to safety and received new supplies of ammunition. The barricade was surrounded, the warriors rested and resupplied. They were ready.

At a signal from Jumper, the forest once again erupted with gunfire. It came from everywhere at once. The blasts of gunfire and cannon mixed with the war cries of the Seminoles. Bullets whistled through the air. The soldiers at the cannon

abandoned their position and jumped back behind the fence. The Seminoles advanced. This time all but three soldiers were killed. Among the Seminoles, only three had been killed and five wounded.

The attack on Dade's troops was only one part of Osceola's plan of attack. Other raids were taking place at the same time. Plantations along the St. Johns River were burned. Crops and stores were raided. Travelers were attacked. The Seminoles wanted the whites to know that they were united and organized. They would fight anywhere and everywhere at once.

One of the raids had a special target—Wiley Thompson. The council of Seminole war chiefs had decided that Thompson would pay for his behavior during the Fort King meeting and for his imprisonment of Osceola. While Dade's troops were under attack by Jumper and Alligator's warriors, Osceola was waiting in the woods near Fort King. With him were about sixty Seminole warriors and some fast ponies.

Through the trees of the forest, Osceola could

see the food supply store, which lay outside the gates of the fort. Through a window, he could see the store-owner and his clerks waiting at the table for their dinner. A big pot of pork, beans, and molasses bubbled on the stove.

An old black woman took the pot off the stove. She began serving the men seated at the table. As the men started to eat, Osceola saw something that made his heart quicken. Wiley Thompson and another officer were walking out through the gates of the fort.

Osceola watched as they strolled toward the store. Would they enter it? Osceola pushed aside a branch and strained to see. But his view of the door was hidden by bushes.

Osceola held his breath and listened. Then he thought he heard Thompson call out a greeting to the store-owner. Without hesitating another moment, he and several warriors rushed the store.

As they reached its door, Osceola let out a loud war whoop. His warriors kicked the door open and shot the owner and his clerks as they sat at the table still eating their meals. The terrified cook ducked behind some barrels and hid.

Osceola ran from room to room with his rifle in hand. But he could not find Thompson. He threw furniture aside and tore open the pantry curtains. Thompson was nowhere to be found. He and his friend had somehow escaped to the woods.

About three hundred yards from the fort, Thompson and the officer hid behind a clump of bushes. The two men could not stop trembling. A twig snapped behind them. They turned to see a Seminole warrior with a rifle in his hand. Then the branches parted, and other armed Seminoles came into view. Thompson and the officer were surrounded.

Shots rang out. Thompson lay dead on the leaf-strewn floor of the forest. Osceola and his warriors quickly raided the store for supplies before leaping onto their ponies and galloping away. They were in a hurry to meet up with Jumper and Alligator. If the battle with Dade's troops was still raging, they would help. However, by the time they arrived, it was nightfall and the battle was long over. A victory celebration was underway.

Osceola showed only brief interest in the celebration. There was too little time to waste on celebrations. He went to bed.

The next morning a messenger brought word that General Clinch was moving troops south toward the Seminole villages along the Withlacoochee River. Osceola gathered 250 warriors and headed south to stop Clinch's advance. In less than half the time it had taken Dade to travel a similar distance, Osceola overtook Clinch's troops.

The sudden arrival of Osceola and his warriors surprised Clinch's force. The Seminoles attacked while Clinch's troops were in the middle of a river crossing. Half his force was on one side, half on the other. In a brief but ferocious battle, both Clinch and Osceola were forced to withdraw. Osceola, though, had succeeded in stopping Clinch's advance.

Safe in the nearby swamps, Osceola, who had

been wounded in the arm during the battle, dictated a letter to General Clinch. He wanted Clinch to know that removing the Seminoles would cost the United States much suffering. He wanted Clinch to consider carefully whether it would be worth the horrible price the United States would have to pay. Osceola predicted that the Seminoles could, if necessary, continue their resistance for five years.

Abraham wrote down Osceola's words. "Say this to General Clinch," Osceola instructed. "You have guns and so do we. You have powder and lead and so do we. You have men and so have we. Your men will fight, and so will ours until the last drop of the Seminole blood has moistened the dust of our hunting grounds."

═◆═ 5 ═◆═

A SHAKY TRUCE

True to Osceola's word, the fighting over the next several months proved devastating to everyone—whites, blacks, and Seminoles.

For a brief time, the Seminoles and their black allies had control of Central Florida. The whites were forced to abandon almost all of their forts and many of their farms and plantations. Then more troops arrived and the Seminoles moved their families into the swamps to escape the soldiers. There, for a time, they were out of harm's way while the warriors battled the army.

But food supplies ran low because there was

little time to plant. Whenever they could, the Seminoles raided plantations, village stores, and army supply wagons. But whites, too, found it hard to farm in this time of war. If the army could not protect a plantation, its crops were carried off or burned to keep them out of Seminole hands. Hunger and sickness were everywhere.

The war dragged on. The longer it lasted the more unpopular it became with many Americans outside of Florida. Its cost in lives and money was, as Osceola had predicted, frightening. Many Americans began speaking out against the war. For some, Osceola even became a kind of outlaw hero. Newspapers carried exciting accounts of his daring deeds.

But among the Seminoles, too, the war was growing unpopular. 1836 was nearing its end, and the fighting had been nonstop for almost a year. Even Jumper, Micanopy, and Alligator were beginning to question the wisdom of continued resistance. Many in their families were sick, some dying. Starvation threatened everyone.

To make matters worse, Osceola was among

the sick. A few months earlier he had caught a fever that came and went constantly. With each passing week, Osceola grew weaker and lost more strength. Others carried on, but his leadership was missed among the war chiefs.

In an attempt to put an end to the war, the United States government decided to pour another two million dollars into the war effort. More troops and supplies were sent south. In December 1836, General Thomas Jesup took command of the troops in Florida.

Jesup began a brutal advance. He was determined to drive the Seminoles south and east toward the Everglades. He searched the swamps for Seminole camps. When he found them, he attacked and destroyed them. Men, women, and children were killed or captured. Survivors fled toward the Everglades. Sickness and hunger continued to claim more and more lives.

By the end of January, Jesup thought the Seminoles might be ready to discuss a settlement. He sent a message to Abraham and Jumper asking them for a truce.

Jesup's battalion was camped at the newly built Fort Dade, and on January 31 the camp was humming with activity. A group of soldiers cleaned muskets near a cypress grove, while others mended uniforms with needle and thread. Two soldiers stood ankle deep in sawdust. Each held an end of a large saw. They dragged it back and forth, cutting an enormous log.

Suddenly a man appeared from behind a clump of mahogany trees. He was carrying a small stick that had been freshly cut in the woods. Tied to one end of the stick was a white flag that fluttered in the breeze. The man looked exhausted. Despite his ragged appearance, he walked in a calm and dignified manner.

The two soldiers stopped sawing. They peered closely at the strange figure. Then they recognized him. It was Abraham.

The soldiers left their saw and ran to tell General Jesup. The general was sitting at his writing desk, which had been placed on the grass under a large tent. Abraham was marched up to the tent. When he reached it, he stuck his white flag into the ground and saluted.

He had come, he said, because he wanted to make one more effort to save his people. Their suffering was great. Many had died or were dying. Some had been living for months on only alligator tails and roots found in the forest. They could not survive much longer.

Jesup studied Abraham. He knew Abraham had influence among the Seminole leaders. But could Abraham convince Jumper, Alligator, and the others to come in to discuss a peace treaty? He promised that he could.

Then Abraham went back to talk to the Seminole war leaders. And during the first week of March, he returned to the fort with Jumper and some chiefs who represented Micanopy. Here they signed a treaty with the whites. By its terms, they agreed to stop fighting. After April 10, all Seminoles in Florida were to come to Tampa Bay where they would be fed and clothed by the army. Then they would move west to Arkansas.

The suffering caused by the war had been so great that for many Seminoles these terms would have been enough. But for Abraham and the other black Seminoles, something more was needed to bring peace. They must keep their freedom. One clause in the treaty spoke to this issue and it pleased Abraham greatly. No one, the treaty said, would be allowed to harm or carry away any black who was allied with the Seminoles.

It looked as if the war had at last come to an end. However, Osceola, who was very ill, was not so sure the war was over. He wondered whether Abraham, Jumper, and Micanopy had made the right decision. Could the whites be trusted to honor their treaty? Would all the war chiefs accept the move to Arkansas? He didn't think so. He didn't want to leave Florida.

Nor was he alone. Arpeika was still against moving, as were Wild Cat and his father, Philip, the great chief of the Seminoles along the St. Johns River. Wild Cat had led many of the raids in Eastern Florida. His reputation had grown during the war until among the war chiefs it was second only to Osceola's.

But rather than take action now, Osceola and

the others decided to remain in hiding in the swamps. Osceola's illness had already caused the Seminoles to lose several recent battles. And as support for the war weakened, so did the influence of the war chiefs. They would wait and see what happened. They would watch the whites and see how well they honored this new treaty. They would rest and see what April brought.

6

ESCAPE FROM TAMPA BAY

After April 10, thousands of Seminoles gathered at two camps near Tampa Bay. They waited uneasily for transport to Arkansas.

The United States government had supplied the Seminoles with clothing and food. They had allowed the Seminole warriors to keep their arms and ammunition. Some still had their cattle as well, which the government promised to buy before the Seminoles left Florida.

Although the war seemed to have ended, peace was uncertain. Many Seminoles still resented the coming move but were too sick or too hungry to resist any longer. Some had only come to Tampa Bay to receive food and shelter, their minds still unsure about leaving Florida. But most of the Seminoles were busy preparing for the move. And there were rumors that even Osceola, Arpeika, and Wild Cat's father were getting ready to come to the refugee camps.

Jesup watched everything closely, worried that something might yet go wrong. And something did. The slave-catchers arrived back on the scene.

How dare he aid in the escape of runaways? they demanded. Slaves were property and should be returned to their rightful owners. They began threatening Jesup, insisting that all runaways should be held until their owners could be found. Jesup didn't really disagree with this. He just didn't trust the slave-catchers to limit their claims to runaways.

As the slave-catchers increased their pressure, Jesup decided to let them into the camps. They would be escorted by his troops to keep their claims in line. First, though, Jesup would meet with the Seminole chiefs already in the camps. He announced to them that those blacks who had joined the Seminoles *after* the outbreak of war had to be delivered up. All others would remain with the Seminoles when they moved to Arkansas.

The Seminoles were furious. To them it seemed that the whites were already breaking their treaty. Jesup didn't see it that way. The treaty, he explained, only promised that the black Seminoles and their free-black allies would be protected from the slave-catchers. It hadn't made any promises about runaways.

The chiefs listened to Jesup but they didn't believe him. The whites had broken their promise. They had been told the treaty meant one thing when they signed it, and now they were being told it meant something else. No, Jesup said, the treaty has not changed. The runaways will have to be turned over.

But before the slave-catchers came to the camps, all the blacks left for the swamps. Their disappearance made Jesup purple with rage. He even threatened to send bloodhounds into the swamps to look for them.

When news of all this reached Osceola and Arpeika, they knew this was their chance. They sent word to Philip and Wild Cat to join them in the swamps. The war would continue. Then they began planning a raid on Tampa Bay. They wanted to convince their people to leave the camps, and then secretly sneak them out. But they realized they would need the help of Abraham to keep Jesup occupied.

While Osceola organized the raid, Abraham was in regular contact with Jesup. He met with Jesup and other camp officials, pretending to make final arrangements for the journey west. He gave no sign that anything had changed. The other Seminoles said and did nothing to arouse new suspicion. They continued to prepare for the move.

On the night of June 2, 1837, Micanopy, Jumper, and Alligator went to bed at their campsite near Tampa Bay. All three had worked hard to keep the Seminoles in Florida. But the white government would not allow it. The Seminoles must move or be killed. Jumper had asked if the Seminoles might stay in Florida if they moved south where no whites lived. Jesup, though, dismissed the idea. He gave them no choice. They must move or die, and too many had already died.

After climbing into his blankets, Jumper lay on his back, watching the dying fire. Sorrow filled his heart. He had done all he could but it had not been enough. The shadows faded with the fire, and the darkness deepened around him. Slowly, mournfully, he drifted toward sleep.

Around midnight, Micanopy was awakened by a tug on his leg. His blankets were ripped away. He sat up with a start and gazed around in alarm. Despite the darkness, he could make out the faces of Arpeika and Osceola.

A few feet away, he saw Jumper. His arms had been pinned to the ground by Arpeika's and Osceola's men. A group of armed warriors formed a circle around them.

"You are surrounded," whispered Osceola to Micanopy. "You will come with us."

"I gave my word to go west," said Micanopy. "I must keep my word."

"Come with us or be killed," said Arpeika.

Little by little, Osceola, Arpeika, and their warriors roused the other Seminole refugees sleeping at the campsite. The entire camp packed their belongings and slipped into the forest. Then they made their way through the swamps toward the north. Here food had been hidden for them.

Over nine hundred Seminole men, women, and children escaped from the camps at Tampa Bay. After they had collected the food and rested, Osceola instructed them to scatter throughout Central Florida. They were to form new settlements in the swamps.

The flight from Tampa Bay opened another chapter of the war. A frustrated Jesup wrote to the Secretary of War for more help. "We have at no former period of our history had to contend with so formidable an enemy," he told the Secretary. "No Seminole proves false to his country. Nor has a single instance ever occurred of a first rate warrior having surrendered."

Despite his respect for their determination, Jesup did not soften his stance. Instead, he vowed that he would defeat them by any means necessary. Following a summer of fierce warfare, Jesup found the means he was seeking.

Wild Cat's father had been captured in a September battle. Under a flag of truce, Wild Cat came to check on his father's condition. Instead of honoring the flag of truce, the army seized Wild Cat. Jesup said he would be released only if he brought Osceola in to talk peace.

A meeting was arranged for the morning of October 21, 1837. Osceola arrived beneath a white flag. A group of officers waited as he walked slowly toward them. His back was straight and his stride, despite months of illness, was steady. The morning sun rose slowly, casting long shadows on the flat ground.

Osceola didn't trust Jesup or the officers who awaited him. He knew how Wild Cat had been captured. But he was willing to risk his freedom for his people. He would talk to Jesup's men. Maybe they were now ready to let the Seminoles move farther south as Jumper had suggested. They would stay in Florida but away from the white people.

Osceola stopped before the officers. Little was said by way of greeting. Osceola stared at the officer in charge, who began reading a letter to Osceola from Jesup. While he did so, 250 soldiers quietly surrounded the camp. Jesup's letter included many questions for Osceola. Why hadn't he prepared to leave for Arkansas? Why hadn't he surrendered the runaways with him? Osceola remained silent. The questions continued until the troops suddenly rushed in.

Osceola had been betrayed by Jesup. He and those with him were captured and sent to a military prison near St. Augustine.

Osceola spent the few remaining months of his life in prison. Wild Cat and several other Seminole warriors escaped on November 29, 1837. Osceola could have joined the escape, but refused. He was too sick. Instead, Osceola and a

number of other prisoners were moved to Fort Moultrie in South Carolina. There his illness grew worse, and within a few weeks, he died.

His gravestone, which lies near the entrance to the fort in which he had been imprisoned, reads:

OSCEOLA
PATRIOT AND WARRIOR
DIED AT FORT MOULTRIE
JANUARY 30TH, 1838

EPILOGUE

Before and after his death, Osceola was a legendary figure to whites, blacks, and Native Americans alike. George Catlin, the famous American artist, painted Osceola's portrait when he visited him in prison. The portrait shows him as a still handsome warrior wearing three ostrich feathers on his head and a turban of many colors.

On February 25, 1839, Abraham moved west. There he sometimes helped with negotiations among the Seminoles, Creeks, and the United States government. But mostly he led a quiet life as a cattle rancher until his death sometime after 1870.

The war between Seminoles and whites dragged on until August 1842. By this time, many Seminoles had already moved west, though the land they moved to was now part of the Oklahoma Territory. Here some prospered while others came into conflict with the Creeks and the whites living there, or with each other. Little by little, their land holdings were chipped away by the Oklahoma land rush.

The Seminole tribe never abandoned Florida completely. A small group that included Alligator, Wild Cat, and Arpeika, under the leadership of Chief Billy Bowlegs, remained in the Everglades. This group developed into the Seminoles of today, who live on the Big Cypress, Brighton, and Hollywood reservations in Florida.

To this day, the Seminoles have never signed a formal peace treaty with the United States. Although they are now citizens of the United States, they have kept their faith in their own culture and in their identity as a separate nation.

Afterword

The Seminoles did not have a written language. Reports of what occurred before, during, and after the Seminole Wars all come from whites and were written in English. When Seminoles' conversations are quoted in such sources, they are translations or interpretations of what the Seminoles said. The only other accounts of what happened during the Seminole Wars come from modern Seminoles and were passed down orally from generation to generation.

The quotes in this book come from the written sources. So do the stories of what happened during battles. Facts about life among the Seminoles have been added to certain accounts in this book to make the atmosphere of the time easier for the reader to picture.

Notes

Page 1   Although a Seminole war chief, Osceola had not been born a Seminole. He was a Muskogee Creek born in 1804 in present-day Alabama. He may have been the son of a white trader named William Powell and a Creek woman named Polly Copinger.

Osceola and his family came to Florida as refugees

after a civil war broke out among the Creeks. Adapting to life among the Seminoles was not difficult for him. In fact, the Seminoles were themselves a mixture of Creek and other tribes who already lived in Florida. Osceola understood their customs and quickly learned their language.

Page 6   At the time our story begins, Abraham was a free man, although he had once been a runaway slave. While still a boy, Abraham had escaped from his white owner in Pensacola. Soon after, he became a slave of Micanopy. Abraham was made Micanopy's "sense-bearer." A sense-bearer acted as a chief's secretary, interpreter, and sometimes as his representative.

In 1826 Abraham went with a group of Seminoles to Washington to act as Micanopy's interpreter. When he returned to Florida, Abraham was rewarded for his services and declared a free man. Later Abraham married the widow of a Seminole chief.

Page 14   To this day historians disagree as to why Abraham and some of the other Seminoles who visited Arkansas put their signatures on the paper. Some claim that Abraham and another leader signed the paper because they were bribed. Others maintain that the wording of the paper was changed after everyone had signed.

Regardless, no one chief or group of chiefs had authority to sign for all the Seminoles. How well the United States government understood this is not clear. We do know the government was happy to get any signatures it could on a treaty. And we know that Native Americans of all nations learned not to trust what government agents put on paper.

In addition Native Americans believed that the land on this earth belonged to the Giver of Breath. The idea that words on a piece of paper could pass ownership to anyone was ridiculous and unreal to them.

Page 20   Osceola's influence was based on the fact that he was *tustennuggee,* or war chief. This was not the same as a commanding officer in the white army. A war chief earned respect and acquired followers by distinguishing himself in war or hunting. He had influence, not command. If a *tustennuggee* had a large number of followers, his influence might be great. He might, like Osceola, influence decisions made by the Seminole people, plan a battle, and lead all warriors in a fight.

Page 21   Those who agreed to move peaceably before the start of the war had reason to regret it. As an example, in December 1835, about 500 Seminoles headed toward New Orleans to begin their journey west. Even before they got there, over 50 men, women, and children had died from disease and over-exposure. The survivors traveled by boat to a location near Fort Smith, Arkansas. Then they were transfered to wagons. By the time the Seminoles reached their destination in Arkansas Territory, 142 were dead and many others were in poor physical condition.

Pages 28–34 Such unfriendly visits to the fort were not part of Osceola's usual behavior. Even at this point in relations between whites and Seminoles, Osceola had friends among the white soldiers.

Osceola's closest white friend was Lieutenant John Graham, a twenty-one-year-old West Pointer. Graham often visited Osceola's village, bringing presents for his daughter. Even after the start of the war, Osceola showed concern for his white friends. He instructed his warriors not to harm Graham if they met up with him during a battle. He also asked his warriors to treat the bodies of fallen soldiers with respect and not to scalp or disfigure them.

Page 58 Jesup was in a tough spot over the run-away issue. If it meant an end to the war, he would have let every runaway in Florida leave with the Seminoles. The slave traders, however, insisted Jesup uphold the property rights of slaveowners. Many whites in Florida and the other southern states were in favor of the war *because* of the runaway issue. As supporters of an unpopular war, they had a great deal of influence with the government.

Jesup had tried to keep the slave traders away from the refugee camps by banning all whites from the area who weren't on government business. But the ban created an uproar among Florida's whites, and Jesup withdrew it.

Page 65 Wild Cat described the escape in vivid terms four years later in a book called *Florida War.* According to Wild Cat's account, he and John Cavallo, a black Seminole chief, were being held in a small room with a very small window about eighteen feet from the floor. To reach the window, they cut up some burlap bags given them to use as mattresses and made ropes, which they hid under their pillows. They then pretended to be sick and fasted. After five days, they decided that they were thin enough to climb through the window, and they then made their escape.

Page 69 When Arkansas became a state in 1836, the western part of its territory was not included within the new state's borders. It was onto this land that the

Seminoles and other southeastern Indian peoples were being moved. For a time the region was known as Indian Territory; its borders included the land that is present-day Oklahoma.

In the 1860s, whites began moving in and the territory was divided in half. The western half was called Oklahoma Territory, the eastern half remained Indian Territory. At one point it looked as if both territories might become states (Oklahoma and Sequoyah were to be their names), but in 1907 Congress admitted both territories to the Union as one state, Oklahoma.

Moses Jumper, Jr. lives on the Big Cypress Reservation in Florida. He is the author of *Echoes in the Wind,* a book of poems, and is the director of recreation for the Seminole Tribe of Florida.

Ben Sonder lives in New York City. He is a writer, editor, translator, and screenwriter. Mr. Sonder is also the author of *The Tenement Writer: An Immigrant's Story.*